Contents

Sexual Violence in the United States:
Summary of the Roundtable Proceedings

Sponsored in partnership by
The United States Department of Justice Office on Violence Against Women,
The White House Council on Women and Girls,
And the White House Advisor on Violence Against Women

Executive Summary

One in six women and one in 33 men will be sexually assaulted during the course of their lifetime.[1] However incidents of sexual violence remain the most underreported crimes in the United States, and survivors who disclose their victimization—whether to law enforcement or to family and friends—often encounter more adversity than support. The effects of sexual violence on victims and communities are profound. Survivors of sexual violence are at a higher risk for a number of physical and mental health problems and other adverse life events, including revictimization.[2] Furthermore, with so few offenders held accountable for their actions, sexual violence amounts to a serious criminal justice crisis.

Congress acknowledged the pervasiveness of violence against women and the need to address these crimes when it enacted the Violence Against Women Act (VAWA) in 1994 and reauthorized the law in 2000 and 2005. VAWA is a multifaceted effort to respond to domestic violence, dating violence, sexual assault, stalking, and other forms of violence against women. VAWA changed the legal landscape, creating new criminal and civil enforcement tools for holding perpetrators accountable and for offering victims access to safety and justice.

---

[1] Tjaden, Patricia, and Nancy Thoennes. 2006. *Extent, Nature, and Consequences of Rape Victimization: Findings from the National Violence Against Women Survey,* Washington, DC: U.S. Department of Justice, National Institute of Justice, NCJ 210346.

[2] *See, e.g.,* Chamberlin, Linda. 2006. *Assessment for Lifetime Exposure to Violence as a Pathway to Prevention,* National Online Resource Center on Violence Against Women. Accessed December 11, 2010. http://new.vawnet.org/category/Main_Doc.php?docid=301.

In addition, VAWA recognized that, given the powerful social barriers that had kept these crimes hidden, public support for specialized outreach, services, training, and enforcement was critically important to realizing the vision of a society that no longer tolerates violence against women. To this end, VAWA established within the United States Departments of Justice (DOJ) and Health and Human Services (HHS) a number of formula and discretionary grant programs to help communities respond to the needs of women who had been, or potentially could be, victimized by violence. Together, these grant programs were designed to increase criminal enforcement, provide necessary services, and support prevention efforts.

Although VAWA addresses both domestic violence and sexual assault, significantly more attention and resources have been devoted to domestic violence at the national, state and local levels. As a result, sexual violence remains a costly, pervasive, and misunderstood crime.

Recognizing that it is time to turn the nation's attention to the issue of sexual violence, the United States Department of Justice's Office on Violence Against Women (OVW) is launching an unprecedented effort to combat sexual violence in the United States by improving the criminal justice system response, expanding services for victims, and changing attitudes.[3] This effort is a part of the Obama Administration's larger commitment to "coordination and cooperation across the entire government to protect victims of domestic and sexual violence and enable survivors to break the cycle of abuse."[4]

On October 27, 2010, OVW, the White House Council on Women and Girls, and Lynn Rosenthal, White House Advisor on Violence Against Women, convened a national roundtable discussion on sexual violence in the United States.[5] This symposium brought together national and local experts and leaders from many fields to examine barriers to advancing the issue of

---

[3] White House Council on Women and Girls. 2010. *Fact Sheet: Obama Administration Highlights Unprecedented Coordination Across Federal Government to Combat Violence Against Women.* Accessed December 11, 2010.
http://www.whitehouse.gov/sites/default/files/rss_viewer/ReducingDomesticViolence_fact%20sheet.pdf.
[4] Ibid.
[5] The National Council of Juvenile and Family Court Judges provided logistical and staff support for the two-day roundtable discussion.

sexual violence, envision a future in which survivors are better served and offenders are held accountable, and to identify a course of action to achieve that vision. Participants continued the discussion with OVW on October 28, 2010 at the National Council of Juvenile and Family Court Judges (NCJFCJ)'s Center for Education on Violence Against Women.

Roundtable participants included survivors of sexual violence, advocates, law enforcement officers, forensic medical examiners, prosecutors and judges. They represented diverse and underserved populations including tribal communities, the gay, lesbian, bisexual and transgendered community, women of color, men, and others.

Federal stakeholders were present as observers on October 27th and included representatives from the White House, the United States Department of Health and Human Services, the United States Equal Employment Opportunity Commission, the Centers for Disease Control and Prevention, the United States Department of Defense, the United States Department of Education, and components of the United States Department of Justice, including the Office for Victims of Crime, the National Institute of Justice, and the Office of Juvenile Justice and Delinquency Prevention. The October 27th discussion took place at the Eisenhower Executive Office Building, and opening remarks were provided by Susan B. Carbon, Director of OVW; Lynn Rosenthal, White House Advisor on Violence Against Women; Thomas J. Perrelli, Associate Attorney General; and Tina Tchen, Executive Director of the White House Council on Women and Girls. The common message conveyed by these leaders was one of strong commitment within the Administration and across federal agencies to supporting survivors of sexual violence, holding offenders accountable, and ultimately, ending sexual violence.

Over the course of the two days, participants were asked to discuss and respond to a set of questions regarding barriers to advancing the issue of sexual violence, strategies for improving the response to sexual violence at the local and national levels, and considerations for public awareness efforts. Participants brought a wealth of knowledge and expertise to this discussion, and the perspectives and ideas they shared will help inform OVW's efforts moving forward.

Roundtable participants identified numerous barriers to advancing the issue of sexual violence. Key barriers they described included:

- The persistence of "rape myths" and misconceptions about sexual violence, which run counter to the majority of victims' experiences, and make it all the more challenging for survivors to disclose their victimization to anyone, from law enforcement and healthcare professionals to family and friends;

- Relentless focus on victim behavior and characteristics—and lack of attention to offenders—which perpetuate victim-blaming attitudes and help offenders evade sanctions;

- Lack of community engagement, which inhibits public discourse on the issue;

- Failure to account for the historical and current contexts of sexual violence as a tool of subjugation and colonization, in particular as this relates to communities of color;

- The discomfort of professionals and the general public with issues of child sexual abuse and incest, which make it even more difficult for survivors to disclose, attain justice, and seek support;

- Victims' reluctance to report their assaults, given that when victims do disclose, they often face skepticism, blame, and further humiliation from professionals, families, and friends, amounting to what many survivors consider a "second victimization";

- Lack of effective training and education on sexual violence, both for first responders and for communities at large; and

- A dearth of relevant research on sexual violence, and the need for better research and data collection to inform the work of practitioners and policymakers.

Following the discussion of barriers, participants shared their ideas on what they hoped to see accomplished over the next several years to improve the overall response to sexual violence. First, participants called for sweeping criminal justice reform, whereby reports of sex crimes would not be disregarded based on false notions about sexual violence. This reform would also involve establishing uniform language around sexual assault investigations and resolving the cross-jurisdictional barriers that stymie investigations and allow offenders to evade sanctions. For instance, participants recommended that tribal authorities need to have jurisdiction over non-Native offenders on tribal land.

Additional themes emerged from this conversation. Participants called for:

- Alternative system responses and greater access to civil legal remedies for victims;

- A shift in the public discourse around sexual violence—from scrutinizing victim behavior to scrutinizing offender behavior;

- Responsible media coverage of the issue and meaningful engagement of the entertainment industry;

- Greater accountability across the board—at the local, state and national levels—and among all disciplines that address sexual violence;

- Reduction and elimination of rape kit backlogs;

- Focus on prevention and bystander intervention;

- Integration of the experiences of underserved populations—specifically communities of color, gay, lesbian, bisexual and transgendered survivors, immigrant women, American Indian and Alaska Native survivors, and adult survivors of child sexual abuse—into the national response to sexual violence; and

- Greater offender accountability, along with critical consideration of sex offender laws, some of which may actually dissuade victims from reporting, especially when the perpetrator is a family member or loved one.

Finally, given that good research drives good policy, participants called for a coordinated, practitioner-informed research agenda to be supported with federal funding. Several participants framed the need for research as a social justice issue, emphasizing that widely-cited data sources rely heavily on crime statistics—which themselves are based on limited notions of sexual violence—and fail to account for victims who do not report to law enforcement.

Further suggestions offered by participants included:

- Develop community-specific social messaging and innovative public awareness campaigns to address sexual violence;

- Acknowledge secondary or vicarious trauma, meaning the ways in which working with trauma survivors and perpetrators affect service providers;

- Place more emphasis on offender accountability;

- Develop, implement, and carefully evaluate evidence-based programs in all arenas, from prevention to criminal justice response; and

- Ensure parity in allocation of resources and funding for sexual violence efforts, particularly within victim services and among underserved populations.

In closing, OVW thanked participants for contributing their ideas and expertise to this discussion. Follow-up steps were identified, to include the development and dissemination of this report, and hosting a series of smaller, topic- and discipline-specific discussions with other stakeholders.

Overview of the Roundtable

Roundtable participants included survivors of sexual violence, advocates, law enforcement officers, forensic medical examiners, prosecutors, judges and other national and local experts and leaders. They represented diverse and underserved populations including tribal communities, the gay, lesbian, bisexual and transgendered community, women of color, men, and others.

Federal stakeholders were present as observers during the October 27th discussion at the Eisenhower Executive Office Building and included representatives from the United States Department of Health and Human Services (including the Centers for Disease Control and

Prevention), the United States Equal Employment Opportunity Commission, the United States Department of Defense, the United States Department of Education, and several components of the United States Department of Justice, including the Office for Victims of Crime, the National Institute of Justice, and the Office of Juvenile Justice and Delinquency Prevention.

Opening remarks were provided by Susan B. Carbon, Director of the Office on Violence Against Women; Lynn Rosenthal, White House Advisor on Violence Against Women; Thomas J. Perrelli, Associate Attorney General; and Tina Tchen, Executive Director of the White House Council on Women and Girls. The common message conveyed by these leaders was one of strong commitment within the Administration and across federal agencies to supporting survivors of sexual violence, holding offenders accountable, and ultimately, ending sexual violence. Following opening remarks, OVW staff, including Associate Director Darlene Johnson and Senior Program Specialist Melissa Schmisek, facilitated a discussion around why it is difficult to advance the issue of sexual violence and what changes the field would like to see in the future.

On October 28, 2010, a three-hour discussion was held at the Center for Education on Violence Against Women, in Washington, DC. This discussion included the national experts and local leaders who participated on the previous day, but federal representation was limited to OVW staff. Director Carbon welcomed the participants, highlighting that OVW's three key priorities around sexual violence are: 1) prevention; 2) reaching out to and serving traditionally underserved victims; and 3) working to change how sexual violence is talked about and responded to in communities across the nation. She called for a "comprehensive, coordinated approach," informed by experts in the field, for addressing sexual violence.

Over the course of the two days, participants were asked several questions designed to explore barriers to advancing the issue of sexual violence, visions for change, and strategies for achieving those visions. This report is a summary of the discussions on October 27 and October 28. It is not intended as, nor is it, a definitive statement on sexual violence in the United States.

Barriers to Advancing the Issue of Sexual Violence

Participants were asked to explain why it is so challenging to advance the issue of sexual violence. Their responses pointed to a number of social, cultural, and systemic barriers, all of which impede efforts to serve victims and hold offenders accountable. Seven themes emerged from the discussion, each of which is summarized below.

Theme 1: Persistence of "Rape Myths" and Misconceptions

The perpetuation of myths about sexual violence—who commits it, who it is committed against, why it happens, and what it involves—reinforces widespread misunderstandings about the issue. Despite the fact that most perpetrators are known to their victims and most sexual assaults do not result in serious physical injury, falsehoods persist that a typical rapist is a strange man lurking in the dark and that rape is not rape unless it involves physical resistance and a great deal of bodily harm in addition to the rape itself.

These "rape myths" run counter to the majority of victims' experiences and make it all the more challenging for survivors to disclose their victimization to anyone, from law enforcement and healthcare professionals to family and friends. Participants also cautioned, however, that stranger rape—while less common than non-stranger rape—*does* happen. Roughly 21 percent of female victims of sexual assault were raped by an unknown offender.[6] The tendency to refer to "the myth of stranger rape" is inaccurate and may alienate these survivors.

Furthermore, participants pointed to a lack of understanding of child sexual abuse and incest as a major barrier to serving victims and securing justice. They described a general aversion among the public and professionals to discussing child sexual abuse and incest, which makes it even more difficult for victims to disclose.

---

[6] Truman, Jennifer L, and Michael R. Strand. 2010. *National Crime Victimization Survey, Criminal Victimization, 2009*. U.S. Department of Justice, Bureau of Justice Statistics, NCJ 231327. Accessed January 24, 2011. http://bjs.ojp.usdoj.gov/content/pub/pdf/cv09.pdf.

Theme 2: Lack of Community Engagement

Participants explained that communities are both unwilling and unsure of how to deal with sexual violence. Many people see sexual violence as "something that happens to other people," and they do not think of it as an issue that is relevant to the whole community. They may be unaware that some of their own family members and friends are victims of sexual violence. What little public discourse exists on the issue is frequently laden with misconceptions and often casts judgment on the victim, rather than the perpetrator.

Additionally, talking about consensual sex is still taboo in many settings, which makes it even more challenging to talk about sexual violence. However, as long as individuals and communities continue to recoil from these challenging issues, sexual violence will continue to be treated as a "private matter" for victims to endure in secret, shame and isolation.

Theme 3: Need for Contextual and Historical Understanding of Sexual Violence

Participants stated that efforts to address sexual violence must acknowledge that these crimes have currently and historically been used as a tool of war and a means of colonizing and subjugating people. As a result, communities within the United States may have different histories related to sexual violence. Without this contextual understanding, efforts to address the problem cannot fully account for the pervasiveness and the multi-generational reality of sexual violence for communities both within and outside the United States. For example, participants mentioned the widespread use of sexual violence by European colonists against enslaved people of African descent and Native Americans. These problems persist today, with some of the starkest examples being the trafficking of women and the use of rape as a tool of war in some parts of the world.

Theme 4: Barriers to Reporting Sexual Violence

Sexual violence remains one of the most underreported crimes in the United States. The Bureau of Justice Statistics reports that the majority of rapes and sexual assaults perpetrated against women and girls in the United States between 1992 and 2000 were not reported to the police.

Specifically, 63 percent of completed rapes, 65 percent of attempted rapes, and 74 percent of completed and attempted sexual assaults against females were not reported to law enforcement.[7] Another study found that only 16 percent of rape victims will ever report their assault to police.[8] When victims do disclose, the responses they receive from professionals—as well as their family and friends— too often involve skepticism, blame and further humiliation, amounting to what many survivors consider a "second victimization." Several participants cited research on victim disclosure and its impact on the healing process, noting that unsupportive and even hostile reactions put victims at a higher risk for developing post-traumatic stress symptoms.[9]

Participants noted that, depending upon victim or offender characteristics and the nature of the assault, some victims face even greater barriers to disclosing. The national and local level responses to sexual violence do not adequately account for the unique needs of victims of color, immigrant victims, gay, lesbian, bisexual and transgendered victims, and other underserved populations. As a result, victims may encounter police, healthcare professionals, advocates, and counselors who—even when well-intended—lack the awareness and skills needed to best serve these victims.

While the law enforcement field has made some strides in improving its approach to sex crimes investigations, participants reported that it is still common in some places for police to minimize crimes of sexual violence and to treat some cases as less serious than others based on victim characteristics and fallacies about non-stranger rape. In addition, participants noted that there is a lack of training for law enforcement officers on how trauma can affect a victim's behavior and her or his capacity to participate in an investigation.

Furthermore, participants explained that prosecutors' decisions to charge or drop cases are inconsistent, and sanctions that amount to a "slap on the wrist" rarely reflect the seriousness of

---

[7] Rennison, Callie M. 2002. *Rape and Sexual Assault: Reporting to Police and Medical Attention, 1992–2000,* Washington, DC: U.S. Department of Justice, Bureau of Justice Statistics, NCJ 194530.

[8] Kilpatrick, Dean G., et. al. 2007. *Drug-facilitated, Incapacitated, and Forcible Rape: A National Study*, U.S. Department of Justice, National Institute of Justice, NCJ 219181.

[9] Kaukinen, Catherine, and Alfred DeMaris. 2009. "Sexual Assault and Current Mental Health: The Role of Help-Seeking and Police Responses." *Violence Against Women* 15: 1331-1357.

the crime committed. When victims perceive that offender sanctions are minimal, victims are further dissuaded from reporting—the added trauma of participating in the investigation and prosecution outweighs any criminal justice benefit for the victim.

Participants also explained that advances in DNA evidence analysis—while presenting many advantages for victims and the legal system—are mistakenly seen as a prosecutorial magic bullet. In many rape cases the dispute revolves not around the identity of the perpetrator, but rather, if the sex act was consensual or coerced. In these cases, the utility of DNA evidence is limited, and it may not be the most critical evidence for moving a sexual assault case through successful investigation and prosecution. For instance, even if a DNA match is confirmed, it is of little use to the case when the accused relies on the "consent defense."

Another institutional challenge is the court system. Even the most flawlessly investigated and prosecuted case may not result in consequences for the perpetrator if the case is presented to a jury—comprised of men *and* women—that holds deeply-entrenched misconceptions about sexual violence.

Aware of all of these realities, many victims feel that reporting to law enforcement would only be time-consuming and retraumatizing.

Finally, some participants cautioned that increasingly severe sex offender laws can in fact dissuade victims from reporting. Particularly in cases of child sexual abuse and victimization by a loved one, a victim will want the abuse to stop but might be afraid to disclose, for fear that disclosure will irreparably damage their relationships with family and friends, and/or that the offender's life will be ruined.

Theme 5: Cross-jurisdictional Challenges

In many under-resourced communities struggling to respond to sexual violence, there is also a need to address cross-jurisdictional issues both in terms of serving victims and holding offenders accountable. The conversation principally focused on Indian Country.[10] Participants suggested that federal agencies responsible for investigating and prosecuting sexual violence in Indian Country need to prioritize these cases and improve the transparency of their processes. Participants also suggested that tribal authorities need to have jurisdiction over non-Native offenders in Indian Country. Native American women are subjected to sexual assault at a significantly higher rate than non-Native women.[11] Participants reported that the vast majority of these crimes are committed by non-Native men on Indian lands. Cross-jurisdictional challenges often allow these offenders to evade accountability.

Several participants contended that cross-jurisdictional issues need not be as complicated as they are sometimes portrayed, suggesting that these matters can serve as needless distractions for law enforcement and prosecutors. For instance, how a particular case may eventually be charged may not need to be decided for an investigation to proceed. Nonetheless, variations in how crimes are legally defined and how cases are handled create challenges for law enforcement and prosecutors.

Theme 6: Gaps in Data and Research

Due in part to the challenges discussed above—including underreporting of sexual violence and lack of community engagement—there are major gaps in data and research on sexual violence. Current research is conducted in silos, and research is rarely disseminated to practitioners in a user-friendly and applicable way.

Additionally, several participants framed the need for research as a social justice issue, emphasizing that existing methods often do not reflect the needs and challenges of underserved populations, particularly communities of color. Participants emphasized the need for more diversity in methods of researching sexual violence, including qualitative and mixed-method approaches, as well as more diversity among researchers themselves. Finally, participants felt

---

[10] According to United States law, Indian Country may include reservations, dependent Indian communities, and allotments.
[11] Tjaden, Patricia, and Nancy Thoennes. 2006. *Extent, Nature, and Consequences of Rape Victimization: Findings from the National Violence Against Women Survey,* Washington, DC: U.S. Department of Justice, National Institute of Justice, NCJ 210346.

that priorities for future research should be the bystander effect and systems' accountability for providing just results.

Theme 7: Need for Education and Training for Communities and First Responders

First responders—meaning those who encounter victims immediately after a sexual assault, such as law enforcement officers and healthcare personnel—often do not have sufficient training on how to appropriately respond and provide meaningful referrals to victims. Participants urged that training for first responders must be practical and relevant to their day-to-day work.

In addition to training for first responders, participants emphasized the need for community education as a means of changing attitudes, preventing sexual violence, and sending the message that sexual violence is never acceptable and will not be tolerated. They urged that a first step is to believe and support survivors.

Next Steps: Where Do We Need to Be in Five Years, and How Do We Get There?

Participants were asked to discuss what they want to see accomplished in the next five years and what strategies could be used to achieve those goals. This conversation flowed directly from the earlier discussion about barriers to advancing the issue of sexual violence. Overall, the most significant priorities participants identified were criminal justice reform, community engagement, offender accountability, and social messaging to change attitudes and shed light on the issue of sexual violence.

Criminal Justice Reform

In discussing barriers within the criminal justice system, participants first noted that laws regarding sexual violence are not enforced adequately or consistently. Participants identified several ways in which the criminal justice system could improve its response to sexual violence:

- The assumption that any rape victim will immediately want to report to law enforcement is false. The criminal justice system must understand the many valid reasons why victims may not want to report before it can take meaningful steps to engage and support victims and thus hold more perpetrators accountable for their crimes. Conversely, victims should be fully informed of potential consequences of delaying a report to law enforcement, since evidence is lost as time passes. While victims may understandably decide not to report immediately, if at all, they should receive objective information from advocates, healthcare personnel, and others so they can make the decision that is best for them.

- Biases against certain victims that lead to some cases being taken less seriously than others must be challenged. Victims' experiences with the criminal justice system vary drastically depending on who the perpetrator is as well as the victim's race or ethnicity, sex, age, sexual orientation, socioeconomic status, relationship to the perpetrator, or occupation (e.g., sex workers).

- It was recommended that tribal authorities need to have jurisdiction over non-Native offenders in Indian Country. As one participant stated, the frightening reality is that an offender can assume: "If I rape a woman on a reservation, nothing will happen to me." They suggested that to address this problem, the field must garner non-Native support for legislation that would give tribal communities jurisdiction over non-Native perpetrators on tribal land.

- Participants urged the United States Department of Justice to issue a set of standard definitions for "false," "unfounded" and "recanted" classifications of sexual violence cases. They cited problems with law enforcement agencies inappropriately using these terms to make decisions whether to investigate a crime.

By and large, participants pressed the need for the criminal justice system to address its persistent failure to hold offenders accountable.

Alternative System Responses

Participants suggested that reform must go beyond the criminal justice system. Ideally, a victim would be able to disclose to and receive an appropriate response from the healthcare, civil legal and educational systems as well as her or his family, workplace, or spiritual community. A more holistic response to sexual violence would promote understanding of survivors' coping mechanisms, particularly those which can make survivors more vulnerable for further victimization, such as use of drugs and alcohol.

Furthermore, victims are often burdened with a number of "hidden costs" of sexual violence, from lost wages to chronic medical issues and healthcare costs.[12] Participants suggested that more civil legal remedies should be available to victims who seek justice and restitution but may not be able to obtain it through the criminal justice system, and victims need greater access to legal representation in civil cases.

Participants emphasized that the healthcare system's response must be strengthened and better coordinated. For instance, more physicians and other healthcare professionals need education on forensic and patient care issues related to sexual violence. Currently, trained forensic nurses provide much of the frontline care for patients seeking forensic examinations, but there are relatively few physicians with high-level training on this issue. The healthcare response can be enhanced—and victims can be better served—if more physicians were equipped with the specific knowledge and skills necessary to provide good forensic medical care, direction, supervision, and leadership.

Finally, an alternative system response could also include expanding advocacy to include more specialized and long term services for survivors.

---

[12] *See, e.g.*, Dolezal, Theresa, David McCollum, and Michael Callahan. 2009. *Hidden Costs in Health Care: The Economic Impact of Violence and Abuse*, Eden Prairie, MN: Academy on Violence and Abuse.

Community Engagement

Participants offered several concrete ideas for engaging communities on sexual violence issues. Their suggestions included:

- Coordinated community responses to sexual violence must focus on holding offenders accountable.

- Efforts to engage communities around sexual violence should imbue the community with a sense of shared accountability, wherein sexual violence is seen as a community problem, not an individual victim's problem. Victims should not be made to feel ashamed; they should be supported by their communities. Social messaging targeted at holding communities accountable (e.g., messages focused on prevention and bystander intervention) can help this effort.

- Sexual violence should be framed as a public health issue.

- Ensure that providers that specifically serve communities of color and other underserved communities have fair access to federal resources to address sexual violence, so that they may develop culturally- and linguistically-specific interventions, prevention, community engagement, public education, and awareness efforts.

- Community engagement efforts should be developed by and for individual communities, rather than foisted upon them. Leaders and anti-violence advocates from the community should be involved in the development and implementation of community engagement and outreach. One participant explained that too often victims of sexual violence are viewed as "other," making it easier to remain unaffected and uninvolved. People become outraged over sexual violence and other injustices when there is a sense of empathy and connectedness in a community.

- Provide resources that support capacity-building among organizations that serve victims of sexual violence, and support ongoing dialogue among advocates through mechanisms such as roundtable discussions.

- Noting that conversations about sexual violence are not happening in many tribal communities, participants suggested developing the capacity of tribal advocates to start these conversations. They recommended gathering a small group of tribal advocates for an initial conversation about sexual violence who would then go back to their respective tribal communities and discuss the issue with the tribal elders. In conjunction with these conversations, a companion guide should be developed for tribal advocates that would guide them in this process.

Social messaging, public awareness campaigns, and other forms of outreach are also a key piece of engaging communities. These strategies are discussed later in this report.

Public Discourse on Sexual Violence and Responsible Media Coverage

Just as communities need to talk about sexual violence, so do local, state and national leaders in politics, media, and other public arenas. Participants did not reach a consensus on how to create this shift, but many agreed that it involves a fundamental change in the way we talk about sexual violence. Too often, public discourse on sexual violence is limited to jokes on television and heavy news coverage of only the most sensational crimes. Furthermore, public discourse fails to acknowledge victims of color and other underserved victims, and fails to account for all of the non-physical and long-term harm that sexual violence inflicts upon a person, including post-traumatic stress symptoms, chronic health issues, effects on spirituality, and other forms of suffering.

In addition, it was mentioned multiple times during both days of discussion that women and girls are perpetually demeaned in advertising and other profit-generating venues. These degrading images of women are commonplace, and the public's reluctance to talk about sexual violence only exacerbates the harm that misogynistic messages do to society as a whole.

Approaches to improving public discourse on sexual violence must include social messaging and responsible engagement of the media. Principally, public scrutiny must shift from victim behavior to perpetrator behavior. Since the media inform the public and can reinforce or challenge social norms, coverage of sexual violence must include a better representation of victims and a more accurate portrayal of the issues. One participant mentioned Counter Quo (www.counterquo.org), a non-profit that seeks to challenge the way media responds to sexual violence, as an example of organizations addressing these issues.

Education and Training for Communities and Professionals

There was a general consensus among participants that communities and professionals need education about, and training on, sexual violence. Some participants urged that education and training should be targeted specifically to law enforcement, prosecutors, healthcare personnel, and other stakeholders who may be involved in Sexual Assault Response Teams (SARTs), as these first responders set the tone for the victim's experience in the criminal justice, healthcare, and legal systems. Legislators would also need to be involved to ensure funding and move education and training efforts moving forward.

Participants identified some issues that education and training should cover, as well as suggestions for implementation. Topics recommended for training and education included: background on all forms of sexual violence; how working with trauma survivors can traumatize the service provider; how to work with survivors who have disabilities or language barriers; how men and women are socialized in ways that foster sexual violence (e.g., how men are expected to be "in control of the situation"); combating homophobia; cultural competency; primary prevention; and sex offender dynamics. Participants also emphasized that curricula and pedagogy must account for the fact that each audience will include primary and secondary survivors who already have personal experience with the issue.

Two strategies to ensure broad access to education and training on sexual violence were:

- Sexual violence education and continuing education for all professionals, paraprofessionals, and emerging professionals in healthcare and mental health fields, as well as for federal and state agency decision-makers, grant managers, and legislators; and

- Implementation of developmentally-appropriate curricula on sexual violence in all public elementary, middle, and high schools, as part of an overall violence prevention effort.

Lastly, it was noted that community outreach is also a way to educate potential jury pools about sexual violence.

Parity and Adequacy of Resources

There was a strong sentiment among participants that there needs to be parity in resource allocation between sexual violence and domestic violence issues. More funding and resources are needed specifically for underserved communities because many rape crisis centers are not reaching everyone who needs their resources. Moreover, if the sexual violence field embarks on a public awareness campaign, adequate resources need to be in place to address the inevitable influx of people who will require community-based services.

Another consequence of rape crisis centers being under-resourced is that these agencies are not able to serve the scores of survivors of child sexual abuse who seek their services. Research has documented the far-reaching impact of child sexual abuse[13] on all aspects of an adult survivor's life. However, given that rape crisis centers are typically resourced to serve only adult survivors in the immediate aftermath of an assault, adult survivors of child sexual abuse have very limited access to the help they need. Funding specifically to serve adult survivors of child sexual abuse could ensure that these survivors are not turned away by service providers.

Accountability

Participants emphasized that efforts to combat sexual violence must focus on holding offenders, systems, and communities accountable. Currently, a great deal of scrutiny and blame is directed at victims of sexual violence rather than the offenders who perpetrate the violence and the

---

[13] Dube, S. R., Anda, R.F., Whitfield, C.L., et al. 2005. "Long-term consequences of childhood sexual abuse by gender of victim," *American Journal of Preventive Medicine*, 28 (5): 430–8.

systems responsible for responding to it. As one participant stated: "The field cannot end sexual violence by only focusing on the victims."

In discussing the need for greater offender accountability, participants also explained that offender treatment should be based on research and provided in a culturally-specific manner to improve its effectiveness. Furthermore, policymakers must take a more critical look at sex offender management and examine well-intended laws that may actually serve to dissuade victims from reporting or increase the likelihood of offender recidivism.

Rape Kit Backlog Reduction

Reduction and elimination of the backlog of rape kits in local and state crime laboratories was identified as a priority. When victims consent to the grueling process of a forensic medical exam, they expect that something will be done with the evidence collected. However, physical evidence from sexual assault cases can sit untested for months, years, and even decades. This crisis allows offenders to evade sanctions, denies justice and safety to victims, and erodes public trust in the criminal justice system.

Coordinated Research Agenda

Given that good research drives good policy, participants called for a coordinated, practitioner-informed research agenda to be supported with federal funding. They urged that more research and better data are necessary to build public awareness about sexual violence and to develop informed strategies for combating it. Research should then be disseminated to practitioners and the public in accessible, user-friendly formats.

Acknowledgment of Secondary and Vicarious Trauma

Throughout the roundtable discussion, participants urged that sexual violence be understood as an issue that has ripple effects beyond the primary victim. Sexual violence affects families, communities, and those who work with survivors and perpetrators. There is a stigma associated with recognizing vicarious trauma in one's life, and first responders can face burnout, compassion fatigue, and frustration with a lack of results, depending on how success is measured. They may feel incapable of continuing the work of supporting survivors, investigating crimes, treating sex offenders, and so forth. Professionals and volunteers who work directly and daily with the issue of sexual violence may become traumatized themselves, and systems must build in mechanisms to support these workers and keep them well.

Public Awareness Campaigns and Social Messaging

In developing a public awareness campaign, the field should consider what it intends to accomplish, and how the campaign will affect sexual violence prevention efforts and services. If the sexual violence field embarks on a public awareness campaign, there will be an increase in people needing community-based services, which will require expanding the capacity of the current infrastructure to handle an influx of requests.

Four public awareness campaign themes were recommended and discussed:

1. ***Start by Believing*** – This campaign, recently launched by End Violence Against Women (EVAW) International, includes a universal message at the local, state, and national levels, designed to encourage public discourse on sexual violence and to promote support for survivors when they disclose. This message challenges myths about rape by confronting the reality that most sexual violence is perpetrated by someone the victim knows, and that many victims do not get the support they need when they do disclose. More information can be found at http://www.evawintl.org.

2. ***Friends and Family*** –While advancing the issue of sexual violence requires that friends and family believe victims, it also requires that friends and family know what to do after sexual violence is disclosed. This campaign would offer words and messages to guide friends and family in what to do next and how to support survivors, particularly when the offender is a family member or friend. Some key strategies include educating the general public about available resources and engaging legislators and faith-based communities in this effort.

3. *Co-survivors and Secondary Victims* – A campaign focused on co-survivors and secondary victims would recognize that those who experience sexual violence indirectly, usually friends and family, can support sexual violence victims, yet there is little information and few resources on how to support co-survivors and secondary victims. This campaign would involve the development and dissemination of resources for co-survivors.

4. *Respectful Relationships* – A campaign to facilitate community education on healthy sexuality and relationships was suggested. Australia's research-based Respectful Relationships campaign for young people was cited as a possible model.

A common theme across recommendations for public awareness campaigns was the need to focus on prevention and bystander intervention.

Technical Assistance

To move the work around sexual violence forward, participants suggested that funding agencies provide more pre-application technical assistance. This technical assistance would help communities: a) determine whether to apply for various grant program funds; b) better understand the scope and implementation considerations for the programs to which they are applying; and c) identify capacity issues to address before applying for funding.

A National Day of Discussion

April is Sexual Assault Awareness Month.[14] As such, OVW asked participants to consider the idea of having a National Day of Discussion in April 2011 that would be followed by a national conference on sexual violence in April 2012. OVW proposed hosting a series of topic- and discipline-specific roundtables between now and April 2011 to inform the National Day of Discussion. Participants were asked to weigh the pros and cons of holding this event and to describe what a Day of Discussion would involve, if plans were to move forward.

---

[14] The Obama Administration was the first to recognize April as Sexual Violence Awareness Month.

Overall, participants embraced the idea of a public awareness campaign, as it would serve as a symbolic event that the sexual violence field could build upon in the future. However, concerns were expressed about the short timeline to convene such an important event, and there was no general consensus about what the National Day of Discussion should look like or accomplish. Given that social messaging around an awareness campaign would have to be developed with a tremendous amount of caution and thoughtfulness, some participants thought it would be better to plan for the Day of Discussion in April 2012.

Participants also discussed whether the National Day of Discussion would be implemented using a "top down" or "bottom up" approach, and what the roles of the federal government and local and national stakeholders would be in its execution. They asked that the vision for the event be clearly articulated and tied to other Sexual Assault Awareness Month efforts. It was suggested that OVW, in conjunction with the roundtable participants and others in the sexual violence field, develop the key messages for the National Day of Discussion, take-aways from the roundtable discussion, and next steps.

Having expressed their concerns, participants provided ideas about what a National Day of Discussion could look like and how to convene such an event. Their ideas included:

- ***Discussions in professional sectors.*** These discussions could be structured, high-level conversations among various professional groups, including the media, healthcare providers, educators, and law enforcement. These smaller discussions would build up to a National Day of Discussion.

- ***On-line discussions.*** These discussions could be encouraged through targeted messages, developed by the sexual violence field and promoted through Twitter and Facebook. A day of on-line discussion would culminate, at the end of the day, in a live web-cast or similar event to address and debrief on the themes of the discussion. A central website could be developed specifically for this day of online discussion. In conjunction with the on-line discussions, T-shirts could be developed with the central website's address, as a way of getting the word out about the day of discussion. However, it should be noted that some tribal and rural communities do not have Internet access or capabilities.

- ***Dinner conversations.*** These conversations could be held over dinners at specific locations, including the White House, churches, bars, or Alcoholic Anonymous groups. The sexual violence field could choose selected dinners for media coverage in magazines, morning news shows, etc. These dinner conversations would "normalize" talking about sexual violence and would reflect that public figures care about the issue. Local communities could be encouraged to host similar conversations.

- ***"Sexual violence affects everyone."*** This phrase was a suggested theme for the National Day of Discussion. To illustrate this theme, the effort could involve high-level people across party lines and in corporate America, to show they are all united against sexual violence.

Closing and Follow-up

OVW identified several next steps it would take following the roundtable discussion: 1) prepare a report of the discussion; 2) host a series of topic- and discipline-specific roundtable discussions; and 3) designate a point person for this project.

Participants were asked to identify topics for future roundtable discussions, identify potential participants for those discussions, and indicate how they themselves would like to be involved in future efforts, if at all. There are multiple goals associated with the series of roundtable discussions, including encouraging discourse on sexual violence in the United States and expanding our capacity as individuals and as a nation to respond appropriately and compassionately to victims of sexual violence and to hold offenders accountable. Suggested groups identified for future roundtable discussions included: law enforcement, forensic scientists, prosecutors, judges, advocates, survivors, men, healthcare personnel, legislators, the elderly, faith-based communities, the sports world, the military, immigrant communities, offender treatment providers, corrections personnel, parole and probation personnel, mental health and trauma experts, the media and entertainment industries, researchers, primary prevention experts, communities of color, youth, and victims from American Indian and Alaska Native communities as well as victims from the gay, lesbian, bisexual and transgendered community.

Ms. Kim Lopez, OVW Program Specialist, was designated as the point person for this project. She can be reached, via email, at Kimberly.A.Lopez@usdoj.gov.

Appendix A: Participants

FACILITATORS

Office on Violence Against Women (OVW)

Susan B. Carbon, Director

Darlene Johnson, Associate Director

Melissa Schmisek, Senior Program Specialist

PARTICIPANTS

Joanne Archambault, Executive Director, End Violence Against Women International, Addy, WA

Elizabeth Barnhill, Executive Director, Iowa Coalition Against Sexual Assault, Des Moines, IA

Claudia Bayliff, JD, Project Attorney, National Judicial Education Program, Falls Church, VA

Connie Burk, Executive Director, The Northwest Network of Bisexual, Trans, Lesbian & Gay Survivors of Abuse, Seattle, WA

Roxanne Chinook, STOP Violence Education Coordinator, Tulalip Tribes Legacy of Healing Program, Tulalip, WA

Michelle Corrao, Director of Community Relations, Prevail, Noblesville, IN

Mark Crawford, State Director, Survivors Network of those Abused by Priests (SNAP), Ebenel, NJ

Kim Day, SAFE Technical Assistance Coordinator, International Association of Forensic Nurses, Arnold, MD

Hon. Mel Flanagan, Deputy Chief Judge, Milwaukee County Circuit Court, Milwaukee, WI

Cat Fribley, Resource Sharing Project Coordinator, Iowa Coalition Against Sexual Assault, Des Moines, IA

Mira Frosolono, Assistant Director, National Center for Rural Law Enforcement Criminal Justice Institute, Little Rock, AR

Rachel Gandell, Public Policy Manager, Rape, Abuse & Incest Network (RAINN), Washington, DC

William Green, MD, Medical Director, California Clinical Forensic Medical Training Center, Shingle Springs, CA

Lynn Hecht Schafran, JD, Director, National Judicial Education Program, New York, NY

Susan Howley, Director of Public Policy, National Center for Victims of Crime, Washington, DC

Neil Irvin, Executive Director, Men Can Stop Rape, Washington, DC

Monika Johnson Hostler, Executive Director, North Carolina Coalition Against Sexual Assault, Raleigh, NC

Maneesha Kelkar, Executive Director, Manavi, Inc., New Brunswick, NJ

Kristina Korobov, JD, Senior Attorney, National Center for the Prosecution of Violence Against Women, National District Attorneys Association, Alexandria, VA

Christine Kryzwonski, JD, National Center for the Prosecution of Violence Against Women, National District Attorneys Association, Alexandria, VA

Aviva Kurash, Program Manager, International Association of Chiefs of Police, Alexandria, VA

Jennifer Long, JD, Director, AEquitas: The Prosecutors' Resource on Violence Against Women, Washington, DC

James Markey, Sergeant, Phoenix Police Department, Phoenix, AZ

Luz Marquez-Benbow, Associate Director, National Organization of Sisters of Color Ending Sexual Assault, Canton, CT

Nicole Matthews, Executive Director, Minnesota Indian Women's Sexual Assault Coalition, St. Paul, MN

Kathy Prudden, LCSW, Adjunct Professor, George Mason University, Alexandria, VA

Holly Ramsey-Klawsnik, PhD, Sociologist & Mental Health Clinician, Klawsnik & Klawsnik Associates, Canton, MA

Delilah Rumburg, Chief Executive Officer, Pennsylvania Coalition Against Rape, Enola, PA

Sarah Tofte, Director of Advocacy and Strategic Partnerships, Joyful Heart Foundation, New York, NY

Michael Weaver, MD, Medical Director, Forensic Care Program, St. Luke's Health System, Kansas City, MO

Kym Worthy, JD, Prosecutor, Wayne County Prosecutor's Office, Detroit, MI

Victoria Ybanez, Executive Director, Red Wind Consulting, Inc., Colorado Springs, CO

Maile Zambuto, Executive Director, Joyful Heart Foundation, New York, NY

FEDERAL PARTICIPANTS*

Mala Adiga, Counsel to the Associate Attorney General, U.S. Department of Justice, Washington, DC

Frances Ashe-Goins, Acting Director, Office on Women's Health, U.S. Department of Health and Human Services, Washington, DC

Constance Barker, Commissioner, U.S. Equal Employment Opportunity Commission, Washington, DC

Kathleen Basile, Lead Behavioral Scientist, Centers for Disease Control and Prevention, Atlanta, GA

Joye Frost, Acting Director, Office for Victims of Crime, U.S. Department of Justice, Washington, DC

Suzanne Holroyd, Communications and Policy Manager, Sexual Assault Prevention and Response Office, U.S. Department of Defense, Arlington, VA

Marylouise Kelley, Director, Family Violence Prevention & Services Program, U.S. Department of Health and Human Services, Washington, DC

Karen Lang, Public Health Advisor, Centers for Disease Control and Prevention, Atlanta, GA

Karol Mason, Deputy Associate Attorney General, U.S. Department of Justice, Washington DC

Emily Miles, Confidential Assistant, U.S. Department of Education, Washington, DC

Thomas J. Perrelli, Associate Attorney General, U.S. Department of Justice, Washington, DC

Catherine Pierce, Senior Advisor to the Administrator, Office on Juvenile Justice and Delinquency Prevention, U.S. Department of Justice, Washington, DC

Kristina Rose, Deputy Director, National Institute of Justice, U.S. Department of Justice, Washington, DC

Lynn Rosenthal, White House Advisor on Violence Against Women, Washington, DC

Tina Tchen, Director, White House Council on Women and Girls, Washington, DC

Kaye Whitley, Director, Sexual Assault Prevention and Response Office, U.S. Department of Defense, Washington, DC

OVW STAFF

Ginger Baran, Program Specialist

Michelle Brickley, Associate Director

Debbie Bright, Program Specialist

Virginia Davis, Deputy Director for Policy Development

Lorraine Edmo, Deputy Director for Tribal Affairs

Bess Evans, Confidential Assistant to the Director

Tia Farmer, Public Affairs Specialist

Anne Hamilton, Program Specialist

Kim Lopez, Program Specialist

Anna Martinez, Senior Policy Advisor

Christina Murray, Management and Program Analyst

Nadine Neufville, Associate Director

Marnie Shiels, Attorney Advisor

Susan Williams, Associate Director

NATIONAL COUNCIL OF JUVENILE AND FAMILY COURT JUDGES STAFF

Erin Hammer, Administrative Manager, Family Violence Department, Washington, DC

Amy Pincolini-Ford, Senior Attorney, Family Violence Department, Reno, NV

Michele Robinson, Project Coordinator, Family Violence Department, Reno, NV

Maureen Sheeran, Director, Family Violence Department, Reno, NV